Fredy Guarín

To the Top!

2012: Transfers to Inter Milán for a multimillion-dollar contract.

2011 The British newspaper *The Guardian* deems one of Guarín's goals (from January 8, 2010, in a Porto-Marítimo match) the best goal of the 2010-2011 European season.

With FC Porto, wins the UEFA European League, a second consecutive Portuguese Cup and a third consecutive Cândido de Oliveira Super-cup.

In March, named Portuguese League Player of the Month and participates in the Copa America in Argentina.

2009 Wins his first Portuguese League title with Porto.

2008 Signs a contract with Portuguese team FC Porto.

2006 A big year: joins the Colombian national team, plays for ASSE (Association Sportive de Saint-Etienne Loire) in France and earns a gold medal in the twentieth Caribbean and Central American Games with the national team in Cartagena de Indias, Colombia.

2005 Plays for Boca Juniors in Argentina and helps the team win the 2006 Closing Tournament.

Wins the Under-20 South American Championships with the Colombian national team.

Takes home third place in the CONCACAF Gold Cup with the Colombian national team.

2004 Signs a contract with the Colombian team FC Envigado.

2003 Participates in the Under-20 Youth World Cup. Colombia wins third place in the competition.

2002 Debuts professionally with Atlético Huila, from the city of Neiva, Huila, in Colombia.

1986 Fredy Alejandro Guarín Vásquez is born on June 30.

Personal File

Name: Freddy Alejandro Guarín Vásquez

Nicknames: Guaro, Freddy

Birth Place: Puerto Boyacá, Colombia

Sign: Cancer

Height: 6 feet (1.83 m)

Weight: 170 lbs. (77 kg)

Position: midfield

Teams Played For: Deportes Tolima, Deportes Taluá, Atlético Huila, FC Envigado, Boca Juniors, ASSE, FC Porto, Inter

National Team Number: 13

Number on Inter Milan: 14

Records: Best goal in the 2010-2011 European season; Player of the Month in the Portuguese League, March 2011

Twitter: @fguarin13

Official Site: www.fredyguarin.com

ISBN-13: 978-1-4222-2655-1 (hc) — 978-1-4222-9196-2 (ebook)

Printing (last digit) 9 8 7 6 5 4 3 2 1
Printed and bound in the United States of America.
CPSIA Compliance Information: Batch #S2013. For further information, contact Mason Crest at 1-866-MCP-Book.

ABOUT THE AUTHOR

Silvia Meave is a writer and journalist. He won the Felix F. Palavicini National Youth Journalist Award in 1992, in Mexico. He is editorial director for the journalistic collective TribuAmericas and works with Yahoo! and Globedia. Meave has published articles in the Mexican newspapers *El Universal* and *El Financiero*, and the magazines *Siempre!*, *Mira*, and *Revelación*. (www.silviameave.net)

Photo credits: EFE/Carlos Durán Araújo: 8; EFE/Luis Efigenio: 16; EFE/Leo La Valle: 6; EFE/Miguel A. Lopes: 22; EFE/Joao Abreu Miranda: 15; EFE/Leonardo Muñoz: 2; EFE/Emilio Naranjo: 19; EFE/Ricardo Maldonado Rozo: 4; EFE/Sebastián Salguero: 24; EFE/Felipe Trueba: 12; Dalayo / Shutterstock.com: 11; Lev Radin / Shutterstock.com: 1, 26

TABLE OF CONTENTS

13

Colombian national team player Fredy Guarín celebrates on November 11, 2011, after scoring against Venezuela in a qualifying match for the 2014 World Cup to be played in Brazil.

Chapter 1

Soccer in the Blood

A LOVING, LOW-KEY AND DOWN-TO-EARTH FAMILY MAN—such is Fredy Guarín, the Colombian soccer player who scored the best goal of the 2010-2011 European soccer season, according to the British newspaper *The Guardian.*

At the beginning of 2010, Fredy was called upon to play for Inter Milan as a loaned player. The move to Italy would prove to be a major personal accomplishment. The young player has come a long way from his native Puerto Boyacá, Colombia.

Born on June 30, 1986, Fredy Alejandro Guarín liked soccer from a young age. The young champion is originally from the neighborhood of Pueblo Nuevo, on the banks of the Magdalena River. It was there that Fredy first dreamed of becoming a star.

Fredy is named after his 85-year-old paternal grandfather, Fredy Miguel, who was the first soccer player in the family.

His father, Walter Guarín, was a soccer enthusiast and played as an amateur. His two siblings also enjoy the sport. By tradition, the family has always been fans of the team The Millionaires. The Millionaires are from Bogotá, the Colombian capital, and have won more national championships in their long history than any other Colombian team.

Fredy was very young when his family left the cattle raising region where he was born, an area close to the mountain range that forms a natural border with Venezuela. They left to live on the opposite side of the country, in Tuluá, in western Colombia.

There, in the heart of the Cauca Valley, Guaro (as his Colombian fans call him) joined the team Deportes Tuluá in First Division C. From that moment on, the young soccer player seemed destined to play as a professional midfielder.

Fredy fights for the ball against his opponent, the Argentine Javier Mascherano (right), on July 6, 2011.

Guarín did not stay in Tuluá long. His parents, Walter and Silvia Vasquez, move again soon after their arrival. This time, they went to Ibagué where young Fredy joined the ranks of the teams Cooperamos Tolima and Deportes Tolima.

Those days weren't easy for Fredy's family. According to remarks he made in 2005 to Camilo Alfonso Pinto, a reporter for the Colombian newspaper *El Tiempo*, Fredy and his family were in the midst of recovering from a great tragedy: the death of Fredy's younger sister, Luisa Fernanda, who had been struck by a car and killed. This painful event would require much time for the family to overcome.

The economic situation in which the Guarín family found themselves upon arriving in Ibagué was also difficult. Fredy's mother needed to work as a maid. Eventually, she had saved enough money to start a clothing business that she later opened in La Burbuja Mall, in the city of Envigado.

Meanwhile Fredy, at eleven years of age, sold empanadas to help his mother pay for household expenses. He also used some of the money to pay for transportation to practice with his team, Cooperamos.

Fast Fact

Fredy Guarín's grandfather, a former soccer player himself, says that even though his grandson scored the best goal in European soccer, he prefers his goal against Brazil in 2003, in the Under-17 Youth World Cup.

For a long time, Fredy alternated classes at his school, La Merced, with practicing for Cooperamos, but "on account of his love for soccer," as the biography on his official websites proclaims, Guarín dropped out of high school in 2009.

It's said that Fredy's grandmother, Mercedes, once explained, "He was left to decide between school and soccer and he chose soccer, and in soccer he's succeeded."

Truthfully, Guarín's passionate dedication to soccer germinated his professional debut in 2002, at just 16 years old, playing for Atlético Huila from the Colombian city of Neiva. His brilliant showing opened the door for his selection to the Colombian national youth team, which was open to players under seventeen years of age.

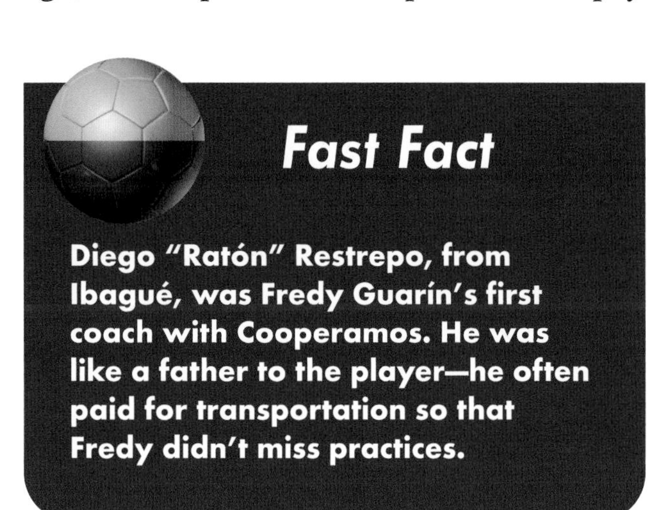

Fast Fact

Diego "Ratón" Restrepo, from Ibagué, was Fredy Guarín's first coach with Cooperamos. He was like a father to the player—he often paid for transportation so that Fredy didn't miss practices.

CELAR LTDA.
VIGILANCIA PRIVADA
SUVECO
POKER
lotto
AGUILA
CAMPEON
SUB 20
SURF

Radamel Falcao García (left) and Fredy Guarín (right), players for the Under-20 Colombian youth national team, celebrate their win in the South American Championships, contested in Colombia on February 6, 2005. Colombia beat Venezuela, two to zero.

Chapter 2

They Didn't Believe in Him

IT WAS FORMER COLOMBIAN SOCCER STAR BERNARDO REDÍN, who scored a goal for Colombia in the 1990 World Cup and later coached for Atlético Huila, who picked Fredy up from the substitution bench of the Colombian national youth team and taught him the secrets of the game.

Recently, in an interview with the Colombian newspaper *El Tiempo*, Redín remarked, "Guarín played as a forward wing." He handled the ball well, Redín said, and above all he didn't run the field just to run around and tire himself out.

Thus, in 2003, the legend of a promising young player in international soccer named Fredy Guarín began.

In August of that year, the Colombian national youth team earned fourth place in the Under-17 Youth World Cup, held in Finland, and two months later that same team took third place in the Under-20 Youth World Cup, played in the United Arab Emirates. In a difficult showdown, they defeated Spain, a team from a nation with a long tradition of soccer and an extensive list of famous champion players.

A year later, the first big chance came for Fredy Guarín to make a name for himself in the professional

Fast Fact

During his stay playing for Boca Juniors, Fredy Guarín polished his technical skills, kicking the ball from more than 100 feet from the net to make "a lot of goals." This practice did not make Argentine soccer coaches happy, but it became the formula with which he helped FC Porto win many games.

Colombian soccer circuit. He signed a contract with FC Envigado, widely known as a hotbed for young up-and-comers. Another former Envigado player who would become a European soccer star like Fredy was James Rodríguez. (Fredy and James later played together for FC Porto in Portugal.)

It's interesting to note that despite being the nest and starting point for many soccer greats, Envigado didn't make any money off of Fredy Guarín, as other teams might have. The team handed the player over to Argentina's Boca Juniors without any financial benefit. "No one thought Guarín would make it," Bernardo Redín has remarked. Nonetheless, after being traded, Fredy played 48 times and scored four goals for Boca Juniors.

Remembering his arrival to Boca Juniors, Fredy commented, "My official debut was in a match against San Lorenzo in Boca Stadium, a match that we lost two to one. I played the entire second half and subbed in for Fabian Vargas."

Ironically, Fredy Guarín was living at that time in the Caballito neighborhood of Buenos Aires, near San Lorenzo's home field in Almagro. Fredy's son, Daniel, was just a few-month-old baby; his new presence in the world a reminder of Fredy's distance from his friends and family in Colombia.

Now, he remembers happily (but without nostalgia) a time when his best friends in Buenos Aires were Colombian compatriots Radamel Falcao García and Fabian Vargas, his teammates; and Jairo Patino, who played for River Plate. They taught him to never stop chasing after his goals in the world of Argentine soccer, where much is demanded of the players.

He also has fond memories of Paraguayan Claudio Marcelo Morel Rodríguez, whom he says is "a good person, an excellent friend, and a great player."

By 2005, Fredy was climbing the ranks of professional soccer. That year, he took home third place in the CONCACAF Golden Cup with his Colombian national team and won another third place victory in

Fast Fact

Fredy Guarín played 48 times with Envigado and scored four goals.

the Under-20 South American Championships. He also emerged from the youth division of Boca Juniors to contribute to the main team's victory in the 2006 Closing Tournament.

Some news outlets from the Argentine press in those years commented that despite being a starting midfielder for Boca, very time Fredy entered out onto the playing field, he showed off the high caliber in his playing technique and a growing sense of what it is to be a goal scorer.

2006 was a great year for Guarín. He joined the Colombian national team, leaving behind his success on the youth squad, and won gold with his Colombian compatriots in the 20th Caribbean and Central American Games, in Colombia.

Even so, no one could have imagined that in such a short time Fredy Guarín would make an even greater professional leap forward—moving up from the prestigious Boca Juniors to the pinnacle of world soccer: the European leagues.

It's said that coach Alfio "El Coco" Basile (photo), wasted his opportunity with Fredy Guarín when he played for Boca Juniors, as he constantly kept him benched.

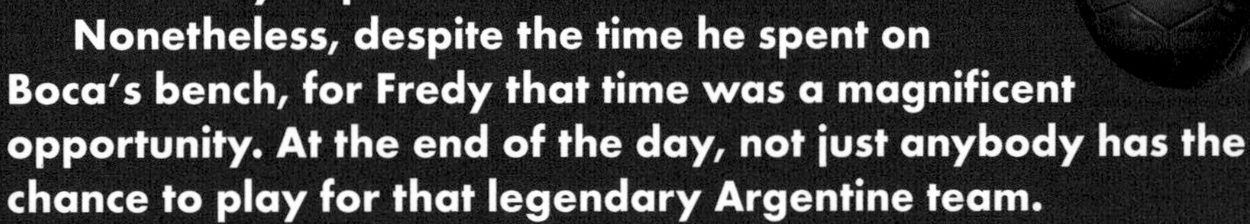

Nonetheless, despite the time he spent on Boca's bench, for Fredy that time was a magnificent opportunity. At the end of the day, not just anybody has the chance to play for that legendary Argentine team.

Various sports analysts recount that Boca Juniors didn't make much of an effort to keep Fredy Guarín on their roster. Other sources affirm that the Colombian player was very clear about his goal to make a career for himself in Europe.

So in August of 2006, the French team Association Sportive de Saint-Etienne Loire (ASSE) from Saint-Etienne, paid the equivalent of 10,500 Euros to have the young winger from Puerto Boyacá on a loaned trade.

His mentor, Bernardo Redín, explains that in those days, Fredy was very thin and experts predicted that he wouldn't succeed among the robust champions of European soccer. Nevertheless, Guarin began his stay in Europe with his right foot forward, and in his first match with ASSE he scored a double against RCD Espanyol from Spain.

It was a friendly match. His debut in France's Ligue 1 occurred on October 14, 2006, in a match against Olympique de Lyon and from that moment on he battled to occupy a spot on the starting lineup with ASSE. His first goal in the French professional league came in a match against Troyes AC.

Moving to France was very difficult for Fredy Guarín. He didn't speak the language and it took him a year to learn it well. However, having the company of his wife and children motivated the young player to keep moving forward.

The Colombian Fredy Guarín (right) drives the ball past Kevin Doyle of Ireland during a friendly match played on May 29, 2008, at Craven Cottage in west London.

In France, Back to the Start

FREDY GUARÍN MET ANDREINA FIALLO, AN ENCHANTING olive-skinned girl originally from the city of Cucuta but living in Medellín, while he was enjoying the sweet taste of success with the Under-20 Colombian national team, and during his participation in international competition like the CONCACAF Golden Cup and the Under-20 South American Championships.

Henry Rojas, a friend of Guarín from their time on Deportes Tolima and Atlético Huila, introduced the couple. In 2005, Rojas was a defenseman for the Under-20 national team, and a friend of the Fiallo family.

Andreina has confessed that she was never a big soccer fan, nor had she ever entered into a stadium, but she does support her national team. Nonetheless, at 18 years old she fell in love with Fredy Guarín and after a brief courtship they formed a family. Currently, they have two children. Daniel Alejandro was born in 2006, and Danna Fernanda was born on Portuguese soil in 2011.

Likewise, Fredy has considered Danna's birth to be a blessing, and a sign of good luck, as her arrival into the world coincided with a series of goals he made that were clutch in his athletic career.

Fredy Guarín's wife accepts the fact that married life hasn't been the easiest, between the couple's young age and the player's constantly changing address.

Andreina has stated that it's difficult to move to countries where you don't know anyone or speak the language, where you have to start from scratch and earn the recognition of the soccer community, and society in general.

According to Andreina Fiallo, at one point, while they were in France, Fredy longed to return to Colombia "where he had several offers," due to difficulties he encountered in trying to earn a spot on the starting squad for ASSE. Instead, he was frequently benched, as was the case when he played for Boca.

Andreina says that she feels fortunate and proud to be the wife on an international soccer champion "because he is a great guy, a marvelous person, and an excellent dad."

In July of 2011, Ms. Guarín stated to *La Opinión*, a Colombian newspaper, that Fredy's biggest dream is to play for Manchester United in England, and follow in the footsteps of championship goal scorers like David Beckham, Wayne Rooney, and the Mexican Javier Hernández.

But while he still waits for that opportunity, Guaro has already established himself with two great teams: FC Porto from Portugal and Inter Milan of Italy. His professional accomplishments will be described in upcoming pages of this book.

Fast Fact

During the 2010-2011 UEFA Europa League, Fredy Guarín scored five goals, ranking fourth among the highest goal scorers in the tournament.

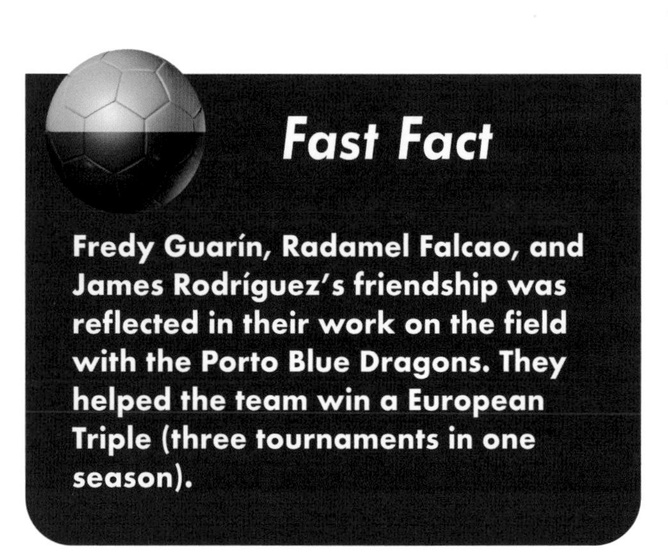

Fast Fact

Fredy Guarín, Radamel Falcao, and James Rodríguez's friendship was reflected in their work on the field with the Porto Blue Dragons. They helped the team win a European Triple (three tournaments in one season).

Preserving His Roots

It can be said that Fredy Guarín matured personally and professionally while playing European soccer. On top of the experience of measuring up professionally against excellent players from around the world—the quickest players with the best skills—he strengthened his body with gym sessions, special training, and rigorous changes to his diet.

Fredy managed to achieve this without abandoning his taste for traditional Colombian cuisine. Those who know him affirm that Fredy would never reject a hearty Colombian dish, nor the chickpea pies from Cucuta that make him feel at

Porto player Fredy Guarín fights for the ball against Leandro Lima (center) of Vitoria de Setubal during a Portuguese League match held in Dragao de Oporto Stadium, Portugal, January 8, 2009.

home even when he is at a great distance from his familiar traditions.

His Colombian roots are strong and his love for his land is deep. His countryman and friend Radamel Falcao García recalls that while they were playing in Europe for FC Porto, Fredy Guarín would "very often" tell his teammates stories about his years in the city of Ibagué. His time living and playing soccer in that Colombian city means a lot to Guarín, as it was there that he experienced some of the earliest highlights of his professional career.

Family, His Inspiration

Guarín would like his son Daniel to follow in his footsteps as a professional soccer player one day. The boy already belongs to his school's team and has a growing passion for soccer already planted in his heart. Still, Guarín clarifies that nothing needs to be forced, as he's still quite young for making such important life decisions.

Even though Fredy left his hometown as a kid, he misses his Colombian family, his grandparents, godparents, childhood

Porto's three Colombian players: Radamel Falcao García (center), James Rodríguez (left), and Fredy Guarín (right), celebrate their Portuguese League Championship victory in 2010-2011. FC Porto defeated Pacos de Ferreira on May 8, 2011, in a match at Dragao de Oporto Stadium in Portugal. The FC Porto club has won the title on 25 separate occasions.

friends, the warm climate, the feeling of his town, and the get-togethers common in his country

Fredy Guarín affirms that his family is his inspiration for moving forward in his soccer career; it's something priceless.

In his free time, while playing for FC Porto between 2008 and 2011, Fredy lived with his teammates and fellow Colombians Radamel Falcao and James Rodríguez as if they were family. Nearly every week they would organize get-togethers and outings, as if they weren't so far from the land where they were born.

During his four season playing for the Porto Blue Dragons, he made strong friendships off of the field with these two Colombian stars, Falcao and Rodríguez. "We're very good friends," Fredy recounts.

A Dream Come True

AS A CHILD, FREDY GUARÍN DREAMED OF SOCCER STARDOM, but he could never have imagined being victorious in Europe. For that reason, he'll always remember the goal he scored as a midfielder for FC Porto on January 8, 2011. It was ranked as the best goal of the 2010-2011 European season in the annual survey released by the British daily *The Guardian.*

It was the last match in the first round of the Portuguese League, and as Guarín has commented time and time again since that day, that goal was a landmark moment for his career and for international soccer as a while.

"It was unbelievable," Fredy started, regarding the best goal of recent years in Europe. In minute 38 of the match between Porto and Marítimo, the Colombian wing shot the ball with his right foot. He bent the ball from nearly midfield and, unstoppable, it went through the goal posts, near the corner. That game ended four to one, with a victory for Guarín's team.

To get to the moment that European and Latin American sports analysts have defined as "epic" in Fredy Guarín's career, three years had to pass since his signing with FC Porto in 2008. In the years he played for the "Blue Dragons," Fredy made other goals for the team's fans of the same magnitude as that infamous shot in 2011; but that time, he claims, the goal was decisive in helping his team raise the Champion Cup in the Portuguese League.

FC Porto signed Fredy Guarín in mid-2008 in a trade that cost the team from Portugal just over one million Euros for a period of four years.

Without a doubt, Guarín was one of the best investments that the Portuguese team has ever made. Throughout his time with the champion Portuguese squad (until late 2011), the Colombian scored eleven goals.

Soccer Career on the Rise

In 2009-10, Guarín won his first Portuguese League title with Porto, and the team won again in the 2010-11 season. He also helped Porto win the Portuguese Cup three years in a row, and the Cândido de Oliveira Supercup in 2010 and 2011.

Previously, Fredy Guarín had won the title of Player of the Month (for March) in the Portuguese League and competed with success in the Copa America in Argentina, with his national team.

It was in the cards for 2011 to be one of Fredy Guarín's best years of his career, playing for FC Porto. It ended with he and his friend Radamel Falcao raising the victory cup in the UEFA Europa League championship tournament. The victory capped off a *trébol* (triplet, in English) for the Portuguese squad—Porto won the league title, national cup, and UEFA Cup.

A goal by Falcao García was the shot (after a midfield play by Guarín) that turned the tables in a match between Porto and Braga Sporting in Dublin Stadium. They won one to zero and the match turned FC Porto coach Andrés Villas-Boas, at 33-years-old, into the youngest coach to ever win a European title.

Fredy Guarín's success with Porto (eight titles, 91 appearances, and 22 goals) boosted his career, as several European teams showed their interest in having the player on their rosters.

Now, Fredy speaks no less than three languages, on top of his native Spanish: French, Portuguese and Italian; an additional achievement in his professional development in Europe.

European Teams Dispute Over a Contract

In 2011, it was said that Juventus, AC Milan, Lazio, and AC Roma de Italia, on top of Real Madrid and Valencia from Spain, all offered contracts worth several million Euros to buy Guarín from Porto. "That's what the press says," the Colombian midfielder affirmed to a journalist, without giving details about what plans were in store for his professional future.

In January 2012, Fredy was loaned to F.C. Internazional Milano, better known as Inter Milan. Inter paid more than 1.5 million Euros for Fredy Guarín to join their ranks for the first six months of 2012. The team had an option to make the transfer permanent for an additional 13 million Euros.

Freddy fights for the ball with Spanish midfielder Pedro Rodriguez during their friendly soccer match at Santiago Bernabeu stadium in Madrid, 09 February 2011.

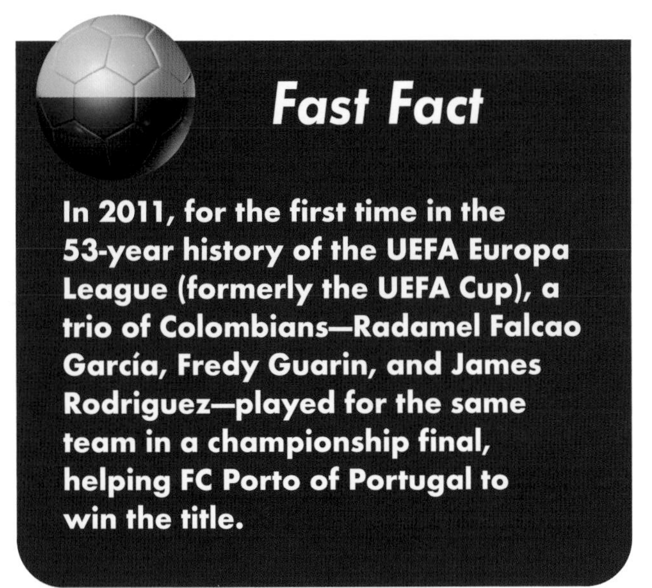

Great Skill and Shot

"I'm a player who, independent of my current standing, is ready to give it all," Fredy has grown accustomed to saying.

Inter Milan, for their part, has been clear in describing Guarín on its website; the reasons for his contract, and the high price they paid for the young wing. They note that he is a center midfielder who knows how to play as a middle or side wing. They highlight his natural right-footed inclination, marked by great skill and a strong kick; a player whose physical strength and strategic skills are his most important assets. He's quick and has a lot of personality, the site clarifies, but above all, Inter's manager remarks, Fredy Guarín possesses much experience and maturity from playing in Europe and with his national team.

Fans in Italy believe that the Colombian arrived at Inter at just the right time, as the celebrated nerazurri ("black and blue," an Italian phrase that refers to the colors of their uniform) has played spectacularly since 2010. As such, Fredy Guarín offers great hope for Inter fans, who hope to see their team crowned European champs once again.

Guaro Returns!

In mid-November of 2011, during a mach between the Colombian and Venezuelan national teams in which Fredy Guarín scored the only goal for Colombian, the wing player suffered a right calf injury, pulling his focus from the national team and forcing him to return to Europe.

The match, allowing the team to accumulate points to qualify for the 2014 Brazilian World Cup, happened in Barranquilla, Colombia, in the middle of a torrential downpour and ended in a tie; but Guarín's showing didn't disappoint.

A curious event in that turbulent match mentioned by Liliana Gama, a Portuguese fan of the Colombian midfielder whom he calls his "Number One Fan" is that: "On the eleventh day of the eleventh month of the year 2011, Colombian and Venezuela tied 1 to 1. Fredy Guarín (his name has eleven letters) scored at minute eleven during the eleventh match for the Colombian squad of that year."

In January of 2012, when Fredy came to Italy to officially start practices with Inter, he was still in no condition to play. There are those who say that Porto staff didn't properly take care of the injury; but other assure that it was most convenient for Inter Milan to allow him to rest a sufficient amount, to start up again in optimal physical condition.

Later on, according to Marcelo Ferreyra, Guarín's agent, the poor climate caused by a cruel European winter prohibited the Colombian from immediately playing his first match with Inter.

Several experts said that Fredy didn't appeared on the field with an Inter uniform right away on account of a rule that the Colombian star from Puerto Boyacá may not play for two different teams in a championship league, and he would have to wait a short while longer to debut in the Italian soccer circuit.

On March 9, 2012, Fredy Guarín announced in Spanish and Italian, by way of his Twitter account, that the day before he had begun training with Inter, posting the hash tag "#Guaro returns," generating much expectation among his nearly 122,000 followers, who want nothing more than to see him in action again.

A week and a half later, he thanked his new Inter teammates and managers for the support they had offered in helped him to adequately recover from the injury.

Ultimately, Fredy played six games with the nerazurri before the 2011-12 season ended. Although he didn't score, he played well enough that most people felt Inter Milan would complete the transfer and have the Colombian midfielder on their team permanently.

Fredy Guarín has spoken with the president of Inter, Massimo Moratti, on a few occasions and both are optimistic about the Colombian wing's future with the Italian team: "I told him that I hope to pay back the faith that he and the teams fans have in men, as soon as possible."

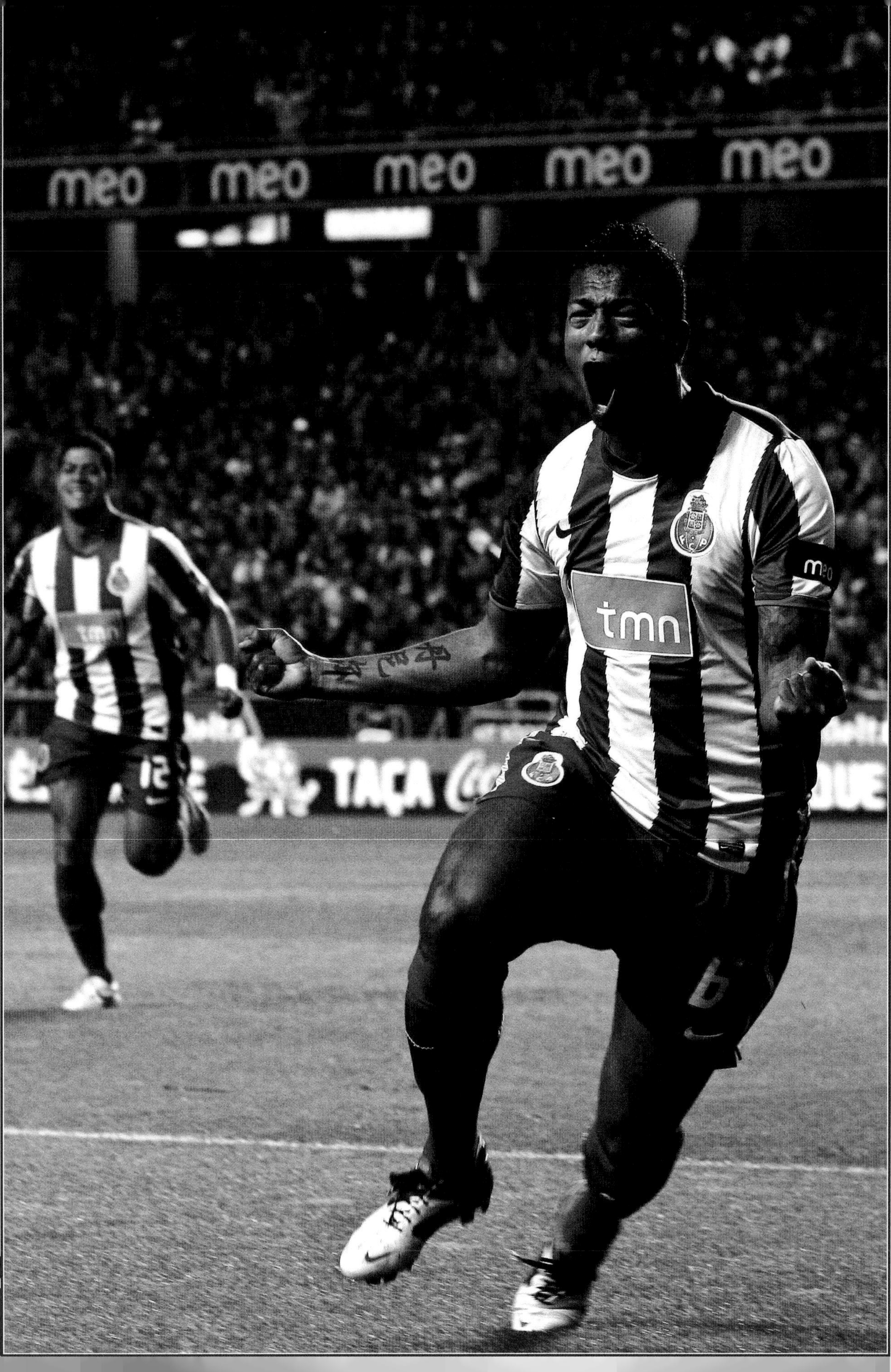
meo meo meo meo meo
tmn
meo
TAÇA

Fredy celebrates a 2011 goal for FC Porto. In January 2012, he transferred to the famous Italian club Inter Milan.

Chapter 5

The Hope of the Nation

COLOMBIA HASN'T QUALIFIED FOR WORLD CUP COMPETITION since their participation in France in 1998. That's why the current coach of the Colombian national team, Hernán Darío "Bolillo" Gómez, has placed his hopes in Fredy Guarín's performance, so that the national team can compete in the 2014 World Cup, which will take place in Brazil.

In less than ten years, Fredy Guarín, next to Falcao and James Rodríguez, has become idolized by Colombian youth. He is a role model for his country. In 2012, he was ranked among the 200 most influential personalities in Colombia, on Twitter, according to statistics from the website Klout, and the number Internet forums created by Latin American and European fans continues to grow. In these Internet communities, Fredy is referred to as "a prodigy of modern of soccer."

Colombian soccer managers are hopeful hat Guarín's participation in national team competition will be a motivator for other players.

In fact, Guarín declares himself a fan of Colombian soccer and claims that he never misses his country's weekend matches, affirming: "We can be the protagonists of international soccer, and we have everything necessary to make that happen."

Fredy, who has appeared in 36 games with the national team and has

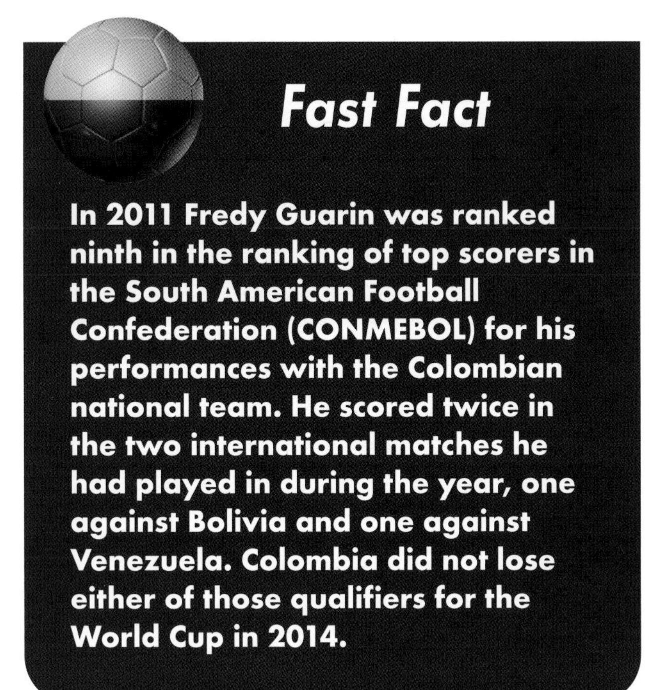

made two goals in international competition, says that he carefully follows the careers of talented Colombians like Dayro Moreno and Macnelly Torres.

In an interview with the Colombian newspaper *El Espectador*, Guarín was asked if he though the national team in his country played as well as FC Porto. Fredy didn't reject the possibility that it could, but he explained that "Porto has a lot of years of experience, the team is always practicing, and that's something the national team is missing: practice time.

A Soccer School

People with a background in soccer who know Fredy Guarín, such as his agent Marcelo Ferreyra, who has worked by his side for seven years, are of the opinion that the Colombian midfielder is a man with his feet firmly planted on the ground, who despite being an extremely valuable player doesn't play only for money, but for the opportunity to do what he likes. That's the key to keep coming out on top.

In May of 2011, Fredy Guarín returned to his native Puerto Boyacá, where his grandparents still live. Government authorities welcomed him and awarded him recognition for representing Colombia and his place of origin in a good way.

The community in his neighborhood of Pueblo Nuevo received him as a celebrity. There was a parade and children saluted him from the sidewalks of avenues, chanting his name.

Fredy has said that he felt moved by his homecoming and promised the population of Puerto Boyacá that he would build a soccer school in his name.

Seeing children with the desire to pursue their sporting interests and build a shining career is motivation for Guarín; it's what he wanted as a child, too.

Guaromania

It has been a long time since Colombia has experienced the euphoria of celebrating their beloved soccer stars, as they now have the pleasure to do.

As with Falcao García's success at Porto and later Atlético Madrid, Guarín has also become the spark for what has come to be called in Colombia an authentic "Guaromania."

On March 15, 2012, just before Fredy's debut playing his first match with Inter Milan at the end of that month, the Italian team announced that the Colombian's jersey would be included in the fan shop Solo Inter in the city of Milan.

Guarín attended an in-store event, where he spoke with reporters. His first words as an Inter player were, "I am content and I feel good. I'm going to return to action soon, I'm almost ready, and I hope to play at the level hoped for by a team like this one."

At that moment, Guarín fans had already grown impatient of not seeing their idol on the field, and social networks were saturated with messages in all different languages, exchanging information about the next steps that they expected Fredy to take in Milan.

The interest in his career was so great that dozens of fans waited outside the store to take pictures with Guarín, or to at least see him up close.

The Colombian player even admitted to being surprised by the show of affection by his new fans in Italy. "I've had the opportunity to speak with some of my fans and they've made me feel very loved," he said. "I hope to be able to help out the team very soon."

Fredy Guarín leaves on a stretcher after being injured, even though he came back to play. The injury happened during a Colombia-Peru match in the quarterfinals of the 2011 Copa America, in Argentina, on July 16, 2011.

Fredy handles the ball during a match against Venezuela.

Masculine Ideal

Fredy Guarín is not only an admired champion, he is also a heartthrob for young girls. The author of this book had the opportunity to meet Liliana Gama, the young Portuguese follower of the Colombian player, since his first days with Porto, who knows by heart all of the details of her idol's life and has met him on more than twelve occasions, on top of having made various videos that she publishes online to show her admiration and affection.

But Liliana isn't Fredy Guarín's only fan. YouTube has an enormous list of videos made by fans, mostly from Colombia and Portugal, who upload songs and messages that speak of the emotions that their favorite soccer player inspires in them.

Love and admiration that young girls profess for Fredy Guarín goes further than considering him a handsome superstar. Liliana summed up what the Inter midfielder represent for young fans of soccer in a moving phrase: "I'm very proud to say that I am a Fredy Guarín fan, because he showed me to never stand down from pursuing my dreams."

Fast Fact

On the internet, Fredy Guarín is number 175 among the most influential Colombians, supported by his 121,300 followers on Twitter, whose numbers grow daily.

On the Way to the 2014 World Cup in Brazil

For Fredy Guarín, the peak of his career still hasn't arrived. Of course, being with his national team in the 2014 World Cup in Brazil is his next goal, but the young idol still has much to prove in the Italian League. It's possible that with his help, Inter Milan will experience a new period of victory both within the borders of Italy and in international competition.

"I'm happy in Milan, it's a city that both my family and I really like," Fredy comments.

The Colombian claimed that he didn't feel pressured to show what he could do on the field because he came to Inter on a six-month loan, and his permanent stay with the team would depend on the team's management. Of course, he gave his best and in May 2012 Inter Milan exercised its option to make the transfer permanent, for a fee of 11 million Euros.

Fredy Guarín always keeps a few Colombian flags in his suitcase, and a traditional hat from his country which he's had the opportunity to show off on the field and during his teams' victories.

The wing from Puerto Boyacá wants to start sporting his flag on the fields where Inter plays, within the next few months, and he shelters the hope and challenge that his national team will make it to the World Cup in Brazil in 2014. "I have a dream I want to make come true. Day by day, I continue to meet the goals I set out for myself," he ensures.

GLOSSARY

assist—when a player passes the ball to another player and that player finishes the play by scoring.

ball possession—action or effect of having the ball, keeping the other team from controlling it.

Champions League—the most important international soccer tournament in Europe.

coach—professional in charge of developing and organizing a team's strategy.

Copa Colombia—also known as the Colombia Cup or the Postobón Cup, an official tournament in which teams from the A and B categories of the professional division of Colombian soccer compete.

Copa Libertadores de América—the most important soccer tournament in the Americas.

counterattack—strategy that consists of making the most of the other team's lack of organization after it has just attacked.

defender—a player who helps to protect the goal area and blocks attacks by the opponent. Within the defense there are various positions: central defender, side defender, and free defender.

extra time—playing time added to the end of a soccer match to make up for lost time caused by interruptions during the match due to fouls, injuries, or warnings.

forward—the player whose mission it is to "attack" (move the ball forward against) the opposite team.

fútbol Sala (futsal)—a game like soccer that is played in a smaller area (often indoors and on a cement floor), with fewer players. It is also known as fútbol de salón or microfutbol.

GLOSSARY

goalkeeper—player in charge of the goal; he is the only one allowed to use his hands in the game.

group stage—stage in the World Cup competition where teams play a short tournament in which the top teams qualify to advance to the knockout round.

jersey—sports clothing that covers the player's upper body and serves to identify the team for which he plays.

knockout round—stage in certain competitions where the team that loses a match is out of the entire competition.

midfielder—player in charge of building up the attack from the middle of the field.

referee—a judge in charge of making sure the rules of the game are followed, and who settles conflicts.

soccer—the term used to describe European football in the United States.

striker—a soccer team's top-scoring forward who usually plays around the center of the team's forwards.

tactics—the strategic plan and soccer philosophy that a coach chooses to employ, after studying the strategies of an opposing team.

UEFA Europa League—formerly called the UEFA Cup, this is the oldest, international European tournament, and is second in importance after the Champions League.

World Cup—most important soccer competition in the world, organized by FIFA.

Triple—occurs when a team wins a league championship, a national cup, and the UEFA Europa League in the same season.

FURTHER READING

Eder Garcés. "Guarin fulfilled his dream." Colombia: LigaPostobon.com (January 31, 2012).

Hector Fabio Gruesso. "Bernardo Redín: Nobody Thought Guarin Was Coming," Colombia: *El Tiempo* (February 3, 2012).

Marcela Angulo Prado. Fredy Guarin: From Puerto Boyaca to the World. Colombia: RCN Television (May 17, 2011).

Jaime Herrera Correa. "Guarin Symbolizes Overcoming." Colombia: *El Colombiano* (July 3, 2011).

Camilo Alfonso Pinto. "Guarin Plays With the Big Boys." Colombia: *El Tiempo* (May 10, 2005).

Guarin, Fredy. "Colombia Is our Pride." Colombia: *The Daily Spectator* (May 19, 2011).

"The Best Goal of the European season 2010-2011" (Video). http://www.youtube.com/watch?v=2WwRNyZTwOM

INTERNET RESOURCES

http://www.fredyguarin.com

Official site of the Colombian soccer player Freddy Guarín, with news, photos, videos and events for fans.

http://www.inter.it

Official website of Inter Milan, with information on the squad's activities, players, stadium, a calendar of events, and an online souvenir shop.

http://www.uefa.com

Official site for the Union of European Football Associations (UEFA), which organizes and coordinates competitions that take place in Europe, such as the European League, Champions League, to European Supercup, and many more.

http://www.fifa.com

Official site for the Federation of International Football Associations (FIFA), which overseas 208 national soccer associations that participate in international competition, including to World Cup. It has news and information about tournaments, teams and players.

http://www.colfutbol.org

Official website of the Colombian Soccer Federation. Information about male and female soccer, local and international tournaments, and indoor and beach soccer.

http://www.fcporto.pt

Official site of the team FC Porto, in the Portuguese Football League, with news, a calendar of scheduled games, info on players, photos and an online souvenir shop.

INDEX